better together*

* This book is best read together, grownup and kid.

a kids book about

a kids book about

ANTI-ASIAN HATE

by Kim Pham

A Kids Co.
Editor Denise Morales Soto
Designer Jelani Memory
Creative Director Rick DeLucco
Studio Manager Kenya Feldes
Sales Director Melanie Wilkins
Head of Books Jennifer Goldstein
CEO and Founder Jelani Memory

DK
Delhi Technical Team Bimlesh Tiwary Pushpak Tyagi, Rakesh Kumar
Senior Production Editor Jennifer Murray
Senior Production Controller Louise Minihane
Senior Acquisitions Editor Katy Flint
Acquisitions Project Editor Sara Forster
Managing Art Editor Vicky Short
Managing Director, Licensing Mark Searle

First American edition, 2025
Published in the United States by DK Publishing, 1745 Broadway, 20ᵗʰ Floor,
New York, NY 10019

First published in Great Britain in 2025 by
Dorling Kindersley Limited, 20 Vauxhall Bridge Road, London SW1V 2SA
A Penguin Random House Company

The authorised representative in the EEA is
Dorling Kindersley Verlag GmbH. Arnulfstr. 124, 80636 Munich, Germany

A catalog record for this book is available from the Library of Congress.
A CIP catalogue record for this book is available from the British Library.
ISBN: 978-0-2417-4396-6

DK books are available at special discounts when purchased in bulk for sales
promotions, premiums, fund-raising, or education use. For details, contact:
DK Publishing Special Markets, 1745 Broadway, 20th Floor, New York, NY 10019
SpecialSales@dk.com

Printed and bound in Slovakia
www.dk.com
akidsco.com

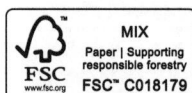

To my family—Maddy, Everett, and Phil.

Intro
for grownups

We all know that hate and racism are bad. What does it look like when an Asian person experiences racism?

Let's talk about it. Let's discuss what hate looks like and how it can make someone feel. Let's learn to recognize these instances and talk about them openly and vulnerably with our kids.

Let's empower our kids to talk about racism. Let's help them find their voices and encourage them to speak up when they see injustice.

Hi, my name is Thu Kim Pham.

But I just go by Kim.

That wasn't always the case.

When I was little, I went by my first name, Thu.*

*It's pronounced like "two."

But kids would often make fun of me because of my name.

They thought it sounded funny.

So I decided it would be easier to go by my middle name, Kim.

That might not sound like
a big deal...

BUT IT WAS TO ME.

I couldn't go by my own name
without someone laughing
at me or pronouncing
it wrong on purpose.

But it wasn't just my name
they made fun of.

It was me.

My food.
(They thought it smelled funny.)

How I looked.
(They said I looked weird.)

Where I came from.
(They thought it was too far.)

And my language.
(They couldn't understand me.)

You see, my parents are both from Vietnam, which means I'm...

VIETNA

AMESE.

I love my culture and heritage.

They're a part of who I am.

And because I'm Vietnamese, I belong to a big and beautiful community known as Asian Americans.

But because of who I am,
how I look, what I eat,
and my culture...

some people can be
really mean to me.

Not just me, but others who are part of my community.

Other Asian Americans.

This is called...

ANTI-
HA

ASIAN

TE.

What is anti-Asian hate?

Anti-Asian hate is when someone is rude, mean, hurtful, or angry at you just because you are Asian.

It can be something that seems small, like when someone says **all Asians are...**

GOOD AT MATH.

BAD AT DRIVING.

QUIET AND SHY.

But saying these things is hurtful because it makes it seem like every Asian person is exactly the same, and we're not.

The Asian community is incredibly diverse!

It's made up of so many different kinds of people from all different countries.

Like...

CHINA, JAPAN, NORTH KOREA, TAIWAN, INDIA, CAMBODIA, MALAYSIA, PHILIPPINES, THAILAND, MARSHALL ISLANDS,

MONGOLIA, SOUTH KOREA, MALDIVES, INDONESIA, MYANMAR, SINGAPORE, VIETNAM, SOMOA, LAOS, TONGA...

Asian Americans are funny, tall, short, smart, and silly.

Some of us like to bake, others like dancing, or basketball, or reading a good book!

We are diverse, unique, and different.

Anti-Asian hate can also be really big things, like telling someone to go back to where they came from.

Or hurting and even killing
someone because
they are Asian.

These aren't things that happened a long time ago...

They happen now.

EVERY DAY.

But growing up, I learned NOT to talk about it.

NOT to bring up the names I was called.

NOT to mention how I was teased.

NOT to share how much it hurt.

In many Asian American communities, kids are taught to...

get good grades,

work really hard,

stay out of trouble,

and be respectful.

We were taught not to speak up when someone was being mistreated—even if that someone was me.

But I have to say
something now.

Because when people do and say these things, whether they're a kid or a grownup, it hurts.

IT HUR

AND

COMM

TS ME.

MY

UNITY.

And because it's never too
late to use my voice...

I'm using it now.

IT'S NEVE LATE FOR USE YOUR EITHER.

R TOO

YOU TO

VOICE

Using your voice can look like many things.

It can be saying something
when you witness
anti-Asian hate.

Or sharing how it
made you feel.

The important thing is
to talk about it.

DON'T IGNORE IT. DON'T LAUGH IT OFF. DON'T JUST HOPE IT GOES AWAY.

AND DON'T PRETEND LIKE IT'S NO BIG DEAL.

Use your voice.

AND STAND UP AGAINST. ANTI-ASIAN HATE.

Outro
for grownups

Racism is hard to talk about—especially with your kids! It's uncomfortable, awkward, and easy to ignore and minimize. So many instances of anti-Asian hate occurred throughout my childhood, and still happen now. I just never talked about how much it affected me...until now.

I challenge you to recall past experiences dealing with or observing racism, and share those with the kids in your life. Talk about how it made you feel and be real and vulnerable with your kids.

We all want to be respected, seen, and heard. Being able to speak up for yourself and others is part of that.

Made to empower.

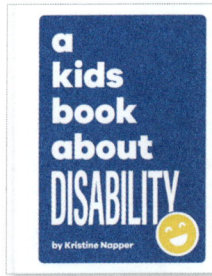

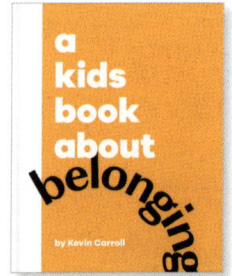

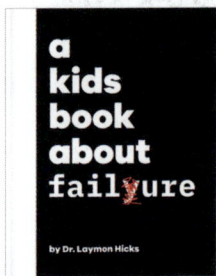

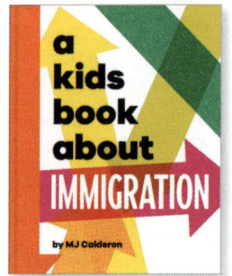

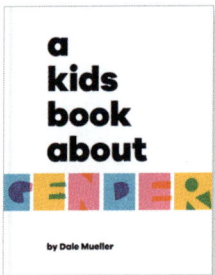

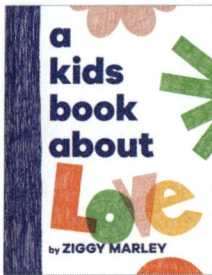

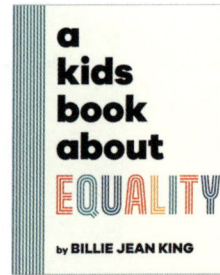

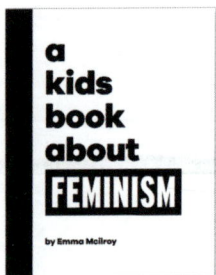

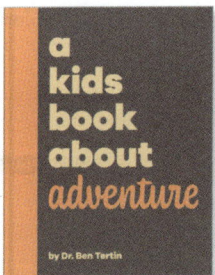

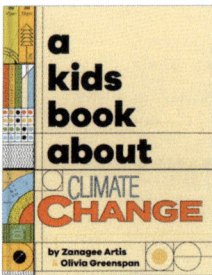

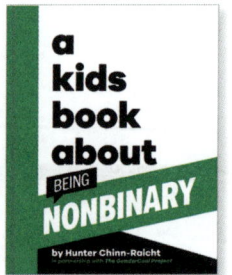

a kids book about **racism**
by Jelani Memory

a kids book about ANXIETY
by Ross Szabo

a kids book about DISABILITY
by Kristine Napper

a kids book about IMAGINATION
by LEVAR BURTON

a kids book about belonging
by Kevin Carroll

a kids book about failure
by Dr. Laymon Hicks

a kids book about GRATITUDE
by Ben Kenyon

a kids book about LIFE ONLINE
by Dave S. Anderson & Blake Fleischacker

a kids book about body image
by Rebecca Alexander

a kids book about IMMIGRATION
by MJ Calderon

a kids book about EMPATHY
by Daron K. Roberts

a kids book about GENDER
by Dale Mueller

a kids book about Love
by ZIGGY MARLEY

a kids book about EQUALITY
by BILLIE JEAN KING

a kids book about MONEY
by Adam Stramwasser

a kids book about FEMINISM
by Emma McIlroy

a kids book about adventure
by Dr. Ben Tertin

a kids book about CLIMATE CHANGE
by Zanagee Artis & Olivia Greenspan

a kids book about CONFIDENCE
by Joy Cho

a kids book about BEING NONBINARY
by Hunter Chinn-Raicht

Discover more at akidsco.com